# From the Bayou to the Phoenix

*By Dr. Alicia Holland*

This book may be ordered through booksellers or by contacting:

iGlobal Educational Services, LLC
13785 Highway 183, Suite 125
Austin, Texas 78750
www.iglobaleducation.com
512-761-5898

Because of the dynamic nature of the Internet, any web addresses or links contained in this book may have changed since publication and may no longer be valid. The views expressed in this work are solely those of the author and do not necessarily reflect the views of the publisher, and the publisher hereby disclaims any responsibility for them.

This is a work of fiction. Names, characters, businesses, places, events, and incidents are either the products of the author's imagination or used in a fictitious manner. Any resemblance to actual persons, living or dead, or actual events is purely coincidental.

From the Bayou to the Phoenix

ISBN-13: 978-1-944346-37-9

# Dedication

This book is dedicated to all the courageous beings who are stepping out on faith to claim their personal power. You are never alone on this spiritual journey. Know that you are loved, you are valued, and you are competent.

# Table of Contents

# *Acknowledgments*

*I* cannot say this enough, but I must give glory to God for helping me realize my potential and purpose in life. Thanks to my editor, Katharine Vail with Polished Printing, who has helped build confidence in my writing skills and challenged me to expand my ideas.

# Chapter 1:
# The Elevator Pitch

*D*uring my first year of teaching, I was on my way to the gym to recruit students into my after-school program. I decided that I would take the elevator to get there faster. My idea of getting there a little sooner quickly faded the moment I found out that the elevator would not open. I became scared and I tried pushing every button possible to make the door open for me to exit, but it would not budge.

I ended up being stuck in the elevator for almost three hours and since I was an elective teacher, no one would notice me because I did not have any students that day. An incredible moment in my life happened while I was in that elevator that day. My relationship with the Lord grew immensely. I started repented of all of my sins and telling the Lord why I was upset. I told Him that I was not happy about being a roving teacher, and I didn't like having an apartment on the third floor, and I had just broke off my relationship with my boyfriend. I was fine with my relationship, but I was not happy about my teaching and living arrangements.

After I had talked to God, I came to terms that I was not in control. As if a sign from above, the elevator miraculously opened and all of the buttons began working. One of my colleagues discovered that it was stuck as she tried to get on the elevator. Even a team of emergency responders and the principal came out of nowhere to help me. It was such an amazing thing to see how God wanted some time to talk to me to help me understand that He had a plan for my life and I had to stop trying to control it.

As soon as the elevator opened, I thanked God and vowed that I would be grateful about any situation because it is a blessing to be alive. To this day, my life has not been the same since because I know that each day is a gift from God.

I learned to be grateful for what I have in my life and what is not ideal is only a learning experience to help us grow into our life purpose using our God-given talents. I knew right then that I had to make a plan for my life, especially my career. I decided that I would work towards a Master's Degree in Education.

About two months later, I was promoted to a classroom and I could not believe it because I thought that was very uncommon in education. God shows up and shows out and that is exactly what He had done in my life.

I learned to be grateful!

# Chapter 2:
# I Found Jesus!

*I* remember going to bed one night thinking about my past, present, and future. Every night, I say my prayers and that one night, the prayer I said was very simple. Use me, Lord, for your Glory. I desire to be used by You. In Jesus Name, Amen. My prayer was short yet effective. I prayed that prayer all that year and even to this day, I still ask the Lord to use me for His glory.

For the first time in two years, God spoke to me that night and I saw him in my dream. He was flying beside me in a white robe and told me that I belong to Him. He said, *"Never forget where you come from."* Where I grew up that meant, "Don't go all Hollywood when you made it out the Hood." I must admit that I still didn't understand it until 2010. Yet, it was living proof that God was real and that was all I realized that I needed. I never considered myself unfortunate because my "hood" taught me everything that I need to know about life. I grew up where the community either corrected you or told on you if you were engaged in any trouble.

The following night, I tried to recreate that dream with God, but I couldn't. I wanted to talk more with Him as I had a few questions this time around. Instead, I started seeing dreams about other people. I had no control over how the dreams appeared, but they just came. I opened my Bible up, and specific Bible verses came about and I just smiled because I had remembered what He told me. My Father in Heaven told me that I was His child! Nothing that I had done or would ever do would change His love for me and my position with Him. When I was ready, I knew that He would keep His promises to me.

I learned that love does not cost a thing, but it requires both oneself and the relationship.

## Chapter 3:
# The Struggle

As I continued to grow in my spiritual journey, my personal journey began to take on hardships beginning with my finances. My girls were one and three and things were finally starting to get a bit easier. The struggle was real with daycare costs. My husband and I were paying for two houses, two car notes, two daycare bills, and expensive electric and cellphone bills.

Through the struggle, we still managed to attend my conference at Disney World in Orlando, Florida. I was twenty-four and it was my first time at Disney World. We were broke, but God made a way for us to have a blast. We ate out of hot plates on the twelfth floor of our hotel for the first week that we were there. Talking about Ghetto Fabulous? We did that!

After the conference, we drove our Chevy Suburban to South Carolina from Florida where the crisis of car troubles began. It seemed like every two hundred miles we had to stop and let our truck cool down. On one of our cool downs, we stopped by Hardee's to get a ham-n-cheese sandwich, and as soon as we got back on the road again, our Suburban died in the middle of traffic.

Again, we stopped to let it cool and got it going again. When we had to stop for gas, we didn't kill the motor in fear of it not starting again. Thank God, the girls were on milk and baby food. We made it to South Carolina and the Suburban died again. My husband and his uncle fixed something under the hood of our truck and we got it working again. We made it safely out of South Carolina and got to Mississippi where we had to kill the motor again for two hours this time. Slowly but surely, our truck, Big Body Baby, was letting us know it was tired.

After two more hours, we started it up, and hit the road again. We made it to Many, Louisiana, to my parents' driveway and the Suburban conked out. My husband's twin brother paid to get it fixed while we ended up staying in Louisiana for three days.

While we enjoyed our family, my husband's job was on the line. We had all of our documentation to reflect car trouble, but it was not enough for him. We later learned that he lost his job the day we made it back to Austin, Texas. My husband blamed me that he was unemployed, which caused strain on our marriage because we were already barely making ends meet.

God showed me that He was in control and that He was my provider. Despite this, look at what God had done for us:

## God's Hand at Work

1. Our bills got paid.

2. We had Supernatural debt cancellation occurred.

3. Our $2500 mortgage was reduced to $1500 a month (Thank you, President Barack Obama).

4. Our children were growing and were provided for.

5. My dissertation was finally approved and I was done in December 2009, but I had to wait until the following semester to graduate in May 2010.

Now, we couldn't go on vacations like we did in the past, but our needs were met and that's all a woman could ask for. Thank you, Jesus, for your grace and mercy upon us.

I was grateful because I had received a doctorate in three years at the age of twenty-six. I knew that this was far greater than me. God wanted to use me, but for some reason, I was not ready. I still wanted to do what Alicia wanted to do, so I continued on that path until my life became one big wreck.

## Chapter 4:
# One Big Wreck

Another hardship in my personal life occurred one morning after I dropped off my two toddler girls at daycare. I thought I was going to make it to work on time for once. My tardiness had been so bad that my principal ended up assigning me lunch duty every day because I missed morning duty and was often late to work. What was I supposed to do?

I was in line under a traffic light headed southbound at a resting position. Out of nowhere, a hummer hit me from behind causing a chaotic scene. I blacked out and all I remember was being in the ambulance with EMTs trying to wake me up. I remember seeing a huge white light. When I woke up, I was at the hospital with my husband.

We had just gotten over being in an argument the night before because he was spending money we didn't have. We had planned for me to stay at home to take care of the girls and for me to finish up my doctorate's degree. I had not planned to stay at home helpless.

After the car wreck, I had to take physical therapy and learn how to use my muscles again. I had just spent eight weeks losing the rest of my baby weight after two years and was a mere one hundred thirty-five pounds. I was back at my high school weight. All of that changed and I became depressed. I went back to emotional eating and in two years time, I gained the weight back and then some. As if my personal obstacles weren't enough, the following year began the downfall of my marriage.

I caught my husband cheating with a married woman. I blamed myself, but that's when my eyes were opened. My life was a wreck because I was in a wreck, both literally and figuratively. For once, I saw what God had been trying to teach me all this time. Without saying, I had given up and was focusing on other things out of divine order. I put everything above God and that was a clear spiritual violation. I began to understand the divine order which included: 1) God, 2) your spouse, 3) your household family, and 4) everything else.

One of the craziest things that I didn't know was that I was free and God had given me a new life. I was caught up with trying to get a new car and get a relationship that I didn't even recognize He had done this for me. In other words, I was trying to be fulfilled with things and people on the outside instead of fulfilling my spiritual need for God. I was an educated twenty-year-old woman who was quite broken and didn't understand who I was spiritually.

I attracted another broken person, who I decided to marry and have my two daughters with. As I look back at my younger self, I cannot be mad at him or myself. That was what I knew at the time. I accepted that and processed how we got together. The one thing that I learned is that you lose people the same way you get them.

As I look at the bigger picture, we were destined to be together at the time. He was my best spiritual teacher. Our souls had a karmic contract and we had already agreed to be together at that particular point in our lives. He wanted children and so did I. We both had goals to a better life and things were going well.

I learned that my daughter was a gift to help me heal my childhood. The Spirit shared this Bible verse with me to help me better understand. *"But women will be saved through childbearing, assuming they continue to live in faith, love, holiness, and modesty."* (1 Timothy 2:15)

I learned that I could still follow my dreams with a family, career, school, and personal life.

# Chapter 5:
# Cheating, Comedy, and Concentration

As I started achieving more of my goals while caring for our children, it seemed like my husband became more and more distant. He worked out of town most of the time so we barely saw each other. I had a classroom teaching job, which confined me to the classroom for eight years.

In 2011, I learned the truth about our marriage. It was a sham! I had been so busy focusing on work, school, and my children that the thought of cheating was just too much for me. I couldn't prove that my husband was cheating until I examined the phone records. As I was doing so, a small voice inside me said, *"Dial that number."*

I called the unknown number and a woman answered the phone. I asked for Jackie and she responded that her name was Liz. My mouth got big and I held back tears.

I apologized for calling and hung up the phone. That same small voice said, *"Call her back."* I called Liz back and asked her how she knew my husband. She immediately hung up. This was the first sign that my intuition was leading me to something I needed to know.

I called Liz back from another number and asked her to listen to me. I told her that my husband was married and she began yelling, "What! He lied to me!" At that point, she opened up to me and shared that she had just had an abortion. She said that she had no clue. I told her that I forgave her and I actually thanked her because she confirmed what I had already thought.

Later that night, I asked my husband if he had anything that he wanted to share with me. He looked me in the eyes and answered no. I said okay and turned over and silently cried myself to sleep. The next morning, I reviewed the records again and saw his boss's number on the phone record. I reverted back to my old self and was ready to find answers.

I grabbed my keys and started up my green jaguar and sped down the toll road. I wanted to get to the bottom of this. I paid a visit to see him at work and he knew that I knew then. He tried to talk me into leaving and I told him it was too late!

While I was at his work, I had a chance to understand another hidden truth. His boss confirmed that he lied. All the times that his boss thought my husband was helping me with the children in the mornings, my husband was going elsewhere. It turns out my husband had hood-winked us both. About two weeks later, he was fired from his job. He blamed me for it. I told him that he was fired for lying to his boss and getting some honey where he made his money. I learned that he was cheating while cooking as he was chef. I had to turn off my mind from it because it was just too much to visualize.

My husband called Liz in front of me and told her that he was leaving me and his family to be with her. She denied him and so did I. After doing more research on Liz, I found out she was married with three boys and was an older woman than me. I told him that he could leave, but after seeing that he wouldn't, I couldn't either.

I decided to focus my energy on something that I could change. So, I focused on writing. For the first time, I felt like I took my power back. After doing what others wanted most of my life, I did what Alise wanted to do and it was simple—share my knowledge with the world.

It became very clear to me that my husband and I were not meant to be. I began to see a pattern of all the men that had cheated on me and the small voice came to me and said, *"This is a generational pattern. You were the last born in your family so you don't know about it."*

I began the quest to learn more about myself spiritually because I didn't like this generational pattern. I wanted to change it, but I realized that I could not do it on my own. For me, Jesus was the answer. I got serious with my faith and repented of my sins. One of the ladies at my church began to mentor me through this transition. I wanted to leave that marriage, but she advised me not to do so. If my husband wanted to work on the marriage then we would try to work through it.

After the pain of him cheating, I wanted to get out of the marriage right away. My husband begged me to stay. There were days I couldn't stand to look at him, but as I reflect on this painful experience, it was never about him. God brought him into my life to teach me, and boy, did He teach me a lot of lessons! That's when I knew that I couldn't stay mad at him forever.

The greatest lesson that my husband taught me was about forgiveness. I had to forgive . . . not only him, but also myself. We agreed to work on our marriage. I came clean with him and shared that I should have waited to marry him until I was completed with what I needed to do for school. I apologized to him because in some way I felt that I had contributed to his choice. I admitted to that much and I saw my mistake.

I learned that I was unequally yoked and had married the wrong man. I began to understand and experience the wrath of being in an unequally yoked marriage. I learned that everything happens for a reason. Spirit is not going to put more on us than we can bear to help us grow spiritually.

# Chapter 6:
# Revenge, Regret, Release, Renew

*A*s I reflected on my pain, I realized that I had to go through the struggles as it could not have been avoided. The stages I went through in my struggles are the following:

Revenge ➡ Regret ➡ Release ➡ Renew

The first stage that I went through was Revenge. I wanted my husband to suffer as much as I did. The problem with that was that I was still not happy, even after I called myself getting back at him.

One night, I prayed and before I could get up that little voice inside me said, *"My child, give your problems to me and read Matthew 6:14-15 and Romans 12:19."*

These Bible verses read, *"For if you forgive other people when they sin against you, your heavenly Father will also forgive you. But if you do not forgive others their sins, your Father will not forgive your sins"* (Matthew 6: 14-15). *"Do not take revenge, my dear friends, but leave room for God's wrath, for it is written: It is mine to avenge; I will repay, says the Lord"* (Romans 12:19).

Even though I found Jesus back in 2006, my relationship with Him had grown. I read those two Bible verses and began to cry. That same voice whispered, *"Luke 7:13, go read, my child."* When I read it, I found, *When the Lord saw her, his heart went out to her and he said, 'Don't cry.'* I promised myself that I would do better. Oh boy, I was being tested . . . daily. I quickly realized that this was a test and I was going through a process. God was changing my heart.

The second stage that I went through was Regret. For the next two weeks, I had a lot of regrets, mainly on the goals that I had set out for myself as a woman. I wanted to be an inspiration to others and especially my children and husband. That voice started again, *"Well, Alise, you still can do all of that. How about you start now? Go and read Habakkuk 2:2."* I read, Then the LORD replied: *'Write down the revelation and make it plain on tablets so that a herald may run with it.'*

When I read this, I knew that my next step was to write down my dreams and how they would look on a daily and monthly basis. This was a period where I had gave up eating and opted to fast. For the next month,

I lost weight and gained better clarity on what I was supposed to do in life. I had a dream and a vision that showed me my life purpose and it was such a heavy assignment, but this time, I saw numbers, pictures, and another Bible verse. The Bible verse was John 14:26, *"But the Advocate, the Holy Spirit, whom the Father will send in my name, will teach you all things and will remind you of everything I have said to you."* I went on and began working on my goals and followed the voice's instruction. Things that I didn't know how to do, the Holy Spirit taught me. I began to put more energy into my work, girls, and relationship with God. I began to notice that my husband's actions did not bother me as much anymore. I knew that what he was going through was issues within himself. It was not my fault so he could no longer blame me. It was time for me to focus on things that I could control. I could not control him or his actions. I learned a secret though, I could control how I responded to him and ignoring him worked wonders!

The third stage that I went through was Release. I felt a little bit better because I learned that this stage was much easier. However, there were still challenges because of how certain situations were playing out. For instance, when my husband lost his job for lying to his boss and sleeping with the woman on the job, it affected our family. Once again, all the bills were on me and God was providing. Deep down inside, I wanted to not work as much.

Well, sometimes, you have to be careful what you wish for as my workload was cut in half and I couldn't afford our $1500 mortgage. I started making choices between eating, lights, and our mortgage. Of course, I chose to eat for our family and I found myself eating more. I knew that it was emotionally eating, but I couldn't do anything about it. The voice came back and whispered, *"Go read Matthew 6:31." I read, So do not worry, saying, 'What shall we eat?' or 'What shall we drink?' or 'What shall we wear?' For the pagans run after all these things, and your heavenly Father knows that you need them. But seek first his kingdom and his righteousness, and all these things will be given to you as well.* I read the verses on my phone and realized that God was in complete control.

We could not afford the house we were living in and I learned that the tenants of what would become our second home were not renewing their lease. We offered to let them out of their lease two months early if they found another house. The tenants searched and were able to find something forty-five days later. Our house went up for short sale and we had several offers, including cash buyers, but it was too late. The bank didn't accept the offer and our house foreclosed without us knowing. A heavy burden was released as every painful moment in that house was now a distant memory. The voice whispered, *"Go read Malachi 3:10." I read, 'Bring the whole tithe into the storehouse, that there may be food in my house. Test me in this,' says the Lord Almighty, 'and see if I will not throw open the floodgates of heaven and pour out so much blessing that there will not be room enough to store it.'*

*"Go Read Philippians 4:19." I read, And my God will meet all your needs according to the riches of his glory in Christ Jesus.*

*"Go Read Luke 16:13."* I read, *No one can serve two masters. Either you will hate the one and love the other, or you will be devoted to the one and despise the other. You cannot serve both God and money.*

After reading those Bible verses, I began to understand where I went wrong. Here's what I discovered:

## My Discoveries

1. I was not tithing like I should have.

2. I was working more than I should have.

3. I was not trusting God as much as I should have with my finances.

I learned that you had to give all aspects to God, not the ones that you think you can handle. The truth is that the work is too heavy for you, as it was heavy for me.

The voice whispered, *"Go Read Exodus 18:18."* I read, *You and these people who come to you will only wear yourselves out. The work is too heavy for you; you cannot handle it alone.*

That is when I made a commitment to give all of it to the Spirit, and I did!

The fourth stage that I went through was Renew. In this stage I learned that my old life was leaving and God was bringing in a new life to me. The thing about it though was that I didn't know how this new life would look. I just knew that I had to let Jesus drive the wheel and put back on my headset to listen to my favorite music. So, I did just that!

I finally had to move back into the house that I had lived before I got married, and things were good. I watched a man try to make it up to me and I was trying as well. I noticed that we got along fine as long as he was not on the phone with negative influences. I had to release that too.

One night, we got a call from Louisiana and we had learned that my husband's mother was rushed to the hospital and two hours later, she died. We hadn't seen her in two years. We couldn't drive there because we had one car that needed repair work and a Jaguar is too expensive to repair. I just had to thank God that the car was paid for and we didn't have a note. My husband ended up having to get a ride to see his family, who criticized me for not coming but the reality was that somebody had had to work in our household.

So, his uncle came to get him and my husband stayed for one week in Louisiana. Finally, the girls and I were able to drive to be with the family. That same day, on our way to Shreveport, Mrs. Alice passed away. We stayed in Louisiana for the next four days because she wanted to be buried quickly. That was the most uncomfortable four days of my life. I finally saw the truth of the matter about his family.

When we returned to Texas, my husband continued to not show any emotions. He hadn't even cried at the funeral. I noticed that he and his twin brother talked on the phone a great deal. My husband seemed to be doing fine and things were back on track. He had got an offshore job in Louisiana and started making a lot of money. He began to stop wanting to pay the bills and wanted to spend more time in Louisiana, making excuses about his job and stating that he was tired to drive to Texas. I didn't stress about it, but I knew that God was not going to let this continue. I did what I had to do for my girls and continued to work on the things that I could control. The Spirit was showing me the truth of the matter. This time around, I chose to accept the truth.

Around March 2013, my mom called me and asked if everything was okay and I said, "Yeah." She shared with me that she saw on social media that my husband's twin brother had a heart attack. I was in complete shock! I started crying because he was only thirty-five and left behind five children. I just could not believe it.

We had just buried my husband's mother nine months earlier, and now his twin brother. The voice came again, *"Go read, Ephesians 5:22-23."* I read, *Wives, submit to your own husbands, as to the Lord. For the husband is the head of the wife even as Christ is the head of the church, his body, and is himself its Savior.*

Even though, we had issues in our marriage, we united as a family unit and I supported him. When I arrived at his family's house in Louisiana, it was a different story. My husband was not himself, but I just let it be. After the funeral, my girls and I drove back to Texas. He drove back to Texas one week later. I didn't bother as I realized that this man was finally grieving and it was important to step away and not focus on our marital issues. I continued my work, caring for my girls, and building both character and faith.

The one thing that I learned when you are in a relationship is it is prone to errors on both sides as we are not perfect. However, when it comes to a relationship with Jesus—if anything goes wrong, it's our fault. It's something that we are doing wrong.

I learned that no one can fix my problems, but God. I had to take the ego out of the way and get with His program. After all, He created me. I learned that I am loved, valued, and competent.

## Chapter 7:
# 9-1-1

In 2013, I finally made the 9-1-1 call. My face was bleeding and I had red marks all over my neck and near my lips from where my soon to be ex-husband choked me. My glasses were thrown off my face and were near the hallway. I couldn't breathe and I was in pain. I ran to the bathroom, locked myself in the bathroom, and dialed 9-1-1. While I was on the phone with the operator, there was a lot of heavy breathing and I felt like I was going to pass out. I forced myself to drink water to keep myself from getting dehydrated. I stayed in the bathroom because I did not know what state of mind my soon to be ex was in.

I was two weeks in recovery from having a tonsillectomoy when he choked me. I had been scheduled to get a tonsillectomy the previous year, but I never had a chance to do it because it required that I took off time from work. I finally went through with the procedure while he was working. We had made an agreement about him taking care of most of the bills for the three months while I was in recovery.

I will never forget how he kept asking me when I was getting my tonsils out. I didn't think anything of it until a small voice whispered, *"You are going to get your tonsils taken out while he is at work. If you need to hire a stranger, then do so!"* That was exactly what I did. I called the doctor and scheduled my appointment. I was very proud of myself because I had ignored the voice for quite some time and you better believe that I had paid for it too.

My main focus for this chapter is to share the spiritual lesson that I learned so that it can help you, if you ever experience any type of domestic violence situation. Please know that there is help in your local area that will help you and they will help you get out of that situation. There are many not-for-profit domestic violence organizations that help both men and women who may experience such a situation. You can get help.

I learned that I was not afraid of change and that my faith was key to the change in which I desired.

# Chapter 8:
# Me, Myself, and Girls

After the abuse I endured, I focused on recovering from my tonsillectomy. I was off work and did not feel well so I just took it easy. The last thing that I wanted to experience was blood gushing from my mouth again which happened as a result from complications of the tonsillectomy.

After about three days of my husband being in jail, he managed to make bail. I later found out that the neighbors had bailed him out of jail. They didn't pay the bail, but they went and got him out. I was furious with them because they had no business getting into our personal situation. They even wanted to take my girls to go see their father. It was at that time that I shared with them that there was an emergency protective order in place and we could not do that. They begged and pleaded with me, but I was adamant at saying no. My girls were my responsibiliy, not theirs. Their actions surprised me, but I knew that I could trust no one but God. This changed our friendship. I realized that these people did not have my best interest at heart and it was time to move forward. I still respected and valued them, but I realized that our purpose was done.

When I received the call from my husband, he shared with me that he was coming back. I told him, "No, the hell you are not!" It was at that time that I had to find a solution. We had just moved back into that house that I had before we got married because he lost his job after his cheating scandal.

Finances were finally looking up and the thought of having to move again into an apartment made me mad. However, when I thought about how the neighbors had done me wrong, I felt that it was for the best. It would allow me the freedom and peace that I desperately needed. After about three days, my girls and I went apartment shopping and they made it clear that they wanted an apartment that had a pool.

I feared for my life because I never thought in a million years that he would hurt me the way that he did. I made up my mind that I was leaving because that was not love and I didn't want to send my girls the wrong message about how men should treat women. The voice came to me and said, *"Go read 1 Corinthians 13:4-8."* I read, *Love is patient, love is kind. It does not envy, it does not boast, it is not proud. It does not dishonor others, it is not self-seeking, it is not easily angered, it keeps no record of wrongs. Love does not delight in evil but rejoices with the truth. It always protects, always trusts, always hopes, always perseveres. Love never fails. But where there are prophecies, they will cease; where there are tongues, they will be stilled; where there is knowledge, it will pass away.*

Immediately, I realized this was not love. Love does not hurt.

## Mansions

After deciding to leave my husband, a leasing agent named Abby helped me find a new place to live. I told her my story and immediately we both began to cry. I shared with her that I was working multiple jobs and child support had not kicked in yet. Abby shared with me that her mother and father were divorced for the same reason. He physically abused his wife. Abby shared that she left her relationship for the same reason and vowed to help me. Abby kept her word with me.

She found us a two bedroom/ two bathroom garaged townhouse by the pool. We loved our little apartment. So, we moved there the week that the girls were on Thanksgiving break. By that time, I had no choice, but to go back to work. Thank God that it was online! Thank God for my parents and sister who provided emotional support. I thanked God because my parents were still here. I was not able to go home as often as I would have liked to, but in due time, they would understand.

About five months later, I learned that Abby had left the apartment complex. Shortly after, the entire leasing staff was let go and I didn't understand why. They were helping people and they cared. I began to reflect on my connection with Abby. I discovered that she was heaven-sent. That voice came and said, *"Alise, Go Read Acts 18:10."* I read, *For I am with you, and no one is going to attack and harm you because I have many people in this city.*

That was all I needed to hear because I knew that God had sent her to help us. Only then, I was at peace. I knew that she had served her purpose in my life and I knew that God was going to take care of her too. It came time for me to think about our next steps and it still felt like I was being held back or something. The energy was off at that place. I didn't like the idea that he knew where I lived because it was literally five minutes from our old house. It was time to move on the west side of town, so we did.

## Austin Canyons

September 2014, the girls and I moved to a better apartment that was still a two bedroom/ two bathroom with a garage, but it had an extra level. We had never lived in a three story townhouse before. So, we were very excited about that opportunity as well. Our lease was for thirteen-months and I knew that we had a place to live. It was located in the Canyon of Austin and it was simply beautiful. For the first time, I felt safe and I didn't share my physical address with anyone. Instead, I used my office address and a P.O. Box.

When it came time for visitations, we met at the mall or another public place. That worked for us. It hurt to see my husband when he saw us. I notice that he was crying. When the visitation was over, I was the one crying, but he just didn't see me. That same month, I had a vision in my prayer meditation, I saw a vision of a school for healing and the name Southwest Institute of Healing Arts came through in my vision as I was in prayer meditation. The voice said, *"Go and read James 4:17."* I read, *If anyone, then, knows the good they ought to do and doesn't do it, it is sin for them.*

I had never heard of this school, but was very excited that I was able to attend the school and get to truly know who I was and why I was here. The Spirit sent this gift the way that I like to learn and educated me with more spiritual knowledge and gifts.

I felt it was time for me to get to know myself and know why I was here. So, I knew that my life purpose had a lot to do with knowledge, but I was always drawn to all things spiritually. I had grown up watching a lot of religious people who didn't even follow their own tenets or some of them created their own religions. For me, I wanted to know the truth so I made a conscious decision to enroll in KC Miller's Spiritual Healing School, the same one that the Spirit showed me in my prayer meditations.

I was accepted into the healing school and was led to concentrate in Spiritual Studies and Specialize in both Spiritual Life Coaching and Hypnotherapy. Through this route, I was able to get ordained as a Spiritual Minister. Two years previous, I had a vision of opening up a healing center, but I had no clue how it would look. I knew that I was on track for my life purpose. I wanted to be a Spiritual Minister who ministered to others through spiritual life coaching. I felt that Spirit planned for me to grow up in poverty and have the life experiences and educational experiences so that I could step into my divine life purpose.

I spent the next eighteen months in school learning about spirituality and getting a better understanding of who I was and why I was here. It was then that I realized that I was to use my spiritual gifts along with my knowledge to serve humanity. For the first time, I found my place in this world. My role was to educate others in all aspects of their life. It made perfect sense why I had such a hard time growing up. It was never about me, it was always about turning my sufferings into service. All of the life lessons and life blessings were meant to be passed on to help others on their spiritual journey.

The highest form of knowledge is spiritual knowledge and when one has both knowledge and character, only then can he or she say that he or she is truly intelligent. Dr. Martin Luther King, Jr. said it best, *"The function of education is to teach one to think intensively and to think critically. Intelligence plus character---that is the goal of true education."*

I was drawn to listening to other Spiritual Leaders and Oprah's Super Soul Sundays and Dr. Iyanla Vanzant's Fix My Life. I began to see the parallel. Oprah had interviewed one of the authors that we were reading about in one of our prayer classes. It was a book on prayers and I knew that the Soul Sundays were exactly what the Spirit ordered. I have always admired Oprah and this show really took that admiration to the next level for me. The Spirit was using her to reach people to the true essence of who they truly are, along with educating them on their spiritual journey.

My girls were more involved in their children's ministry and it warmed my heart at how much they loved God. At first, I must admit that they were upset about the transition and they gave me a little attitude. I was not called to bash their father and I didn't. I was as honest as I probably could be for children their age. I wanted them to use their own creative and critical thinking skills to understand what happened. They were born from love and I wanted them to know that they are still loved by both parents. Children are more forgiving and it was a blessing to see how my Georgia and Amaiya interacted with their father.

I saw two kids who only cared about their father loving them and showing attention. When he was not working, he did. My husband chose me to be the mother of his children, so I would never deny him to see his children.

He told me that he knew that and it actually brought me peace. I shared with him that we get along fine when we focus on our girls and that's what I want to focus on with him. Let's do right by them! He agreed and so did I!

That worked for a little bit. Visitations were going well until the next court case date came about and communication broke down . . . fast!

I learned that I needed to care for myself first before I could nurture others. So, I decided to find out who I was and why I am here. In a prayer meditation, the spirit showed me the perfect school, Southwest Institute of Healing Arts, to refine my spiritual gifts and help me answer the spirit's call.

# Chapter 9:
# Renaissance Rebirth

*I* could not believe that it had been two years since my girls and I moved out on our own. A lot of life transitions happened in 2015 and they were back to back. I only had enough energy to deal with them one step at a time so that's what I did.

In March 2015, I was awarded Sole Custody and Back Time Child Support from two years. The courts kept my address private because I requested it and that can happen if you are a domestic violence victim. In the child support order, it was written that I could move anywhere. I told them if I moved that it would be because of employment. I thanked God after court and was grateful.

The following month, another life transition occurred. This time, we had another court date for the domestic violence that had occurred two years ago. After two years

of trying to persuade me to drop the charges, my ex husband finally realized that I was not going to drop them
because I couldn't. The state picked it up when I dialed
9-1-1. I learned that I did not have to come to court
and that he pled guilty for felony choking and ended up
taking a lesser charge.

He was sentenced to twenty-five days in jail. At last,
the truth came out because for those two years, he had
his family and some of my family believing otherwise. It
was not a time to celebrate this situation, but thank God
that the truth came out and all I had to do was be still.
I still prayed for God to show His face to my ex husband
and lead him on the path in which he is meant to follow.
I was well aware that if I had to learn some tough life lessons that he had to learn some tough life lessons too, and
it seemed as if his lessons were beginning for him. Even
then, I still wished him well, I just wanted to be free from
all of the drama.

Since I had a hard time serving him for child support,
I didn't waste any time with serving him my divorce
papers. In April 2015, I served him my divorce papers
while he was in jail. I later found out that he served about
eleven of the twenty-five days and had to report to work.
Twenty days passed, I didn't have five grand for a lawyer
so I represented myself.

I looked online for free Texas legal help and found the
documents in which I needed and print it out. For the
first time, I was in court. This time, defending myself.
The voice whispered, *"You are not alone."* I just smiled.

As nervous as I was, I followed the judge's order and read my plea statement. The divorce was easy because it was a domestic violence situation and child support had been established. When the judge signed my divorce decree and told me that I was dismissed, I ran out of that courtroom and filed that document. I was officially back to my maiden name again.

## After the Divorce

It was time again to see where I wanted to go next. I went into prayer meditation and God started speaking to me. I got the same message from 2014, *"Move West."* This time, move West meant either Arizona, California, Nevada, or New Mexico. I knew California was out of the questions (for now anyways), but Arizona made sense. I started to think and realized that Arizona was part of my life purpose. I contacted an apartment locator and asked him to find an apartment near my employer. I worked for other colleges and universities, but had been working with clients from the west coast for over ten years. They were thrilled to learn that I was moving out that way. I began to resonate with the slogan, *"I am Phoenix."* I thought to myself that would be nice. My girls and I had already booked a hotel to fly out to my ordination ceremony to officially be ordained as a Minister at the Southwest Institute of Healing Arts (SWIHA). That event was scheduled for December 2015. In the meantime, I was struggling, but was at peace and knew that God would keep his promise to me. He didn't forsake me in the past and he definitely wasn't going to do it now.

After two years of working on myself, building my faith, and raising my two daughters, I was still not ready for a relationship, but I had made friends. People from my past showed up to tell me that they were sorry and I accepted their apology. I apologized to them and they accepted. We laughed at the old times, but it was very clear that we were on different spiritual paths, but I respected them. One of the members from my church shared with me that he adored me for being strong and following God's lead through this season in my life. Those words went a long way and I told him thank you. About two months later, he took me on a date and we had a great time. For the first time in years, I was actually happy and felt desired. We went on several dates and I liked the fact that we had a friendship that did not involve sex. Steve Harvey's words of wisdom came to my mind. "Men are always on." I listened to his morning show faithfully while living in Austin. I wished it was in Phoenix. Steve Harvey educated me and I am grateful for his common sense approach to relationships. While I could not control his actions, I was smart enough to know that he cared about me enough not to violate me in that way. I couldn't ask for anything more. We spent time together the next few months and I dropped a bombshell—I was moving . . . to Phoenix in less than two weeks. I had never seen a man show so much to me. The apartment locator named Steve called me and let me know that he had found an apartment in Phoenix. I had no clue where because I had never been to Phoenix, but I had travelled to Scottsdale about twelve years ago on business. My new love interest and I started seeing each other daily instead of once a week. We started having conversations about the future. I truly liked him and thought that he would be a positive influence on me and my children. It came time to move and I managed to pay for everything one week at a time. I was still waiting on a job offer so I was stepping out on faith when I moved to Phoenix.

## Moving Day

Upon pickup of our belongings. I didn't have much to my name, but the moving company worked with me. Arizona was the perfect place to raise kids. I owed the movers $1900, but only paid $1,000 to get them to pick up the furniture. I thanked God because I knew that it was He who sent this moving company to help us in such a short time.

The girls and I stayed at an Austin hotel. Monty gave me money to ensure that we had what we needed. That next day, he took us to the airport and we kissed each other good-bye and I began to cry. The voice said, *"Go to Psalms 37:4."* *Take delight in the LORD, and he will give you the desires of your heart.* I wiped my tears, took my girls, and checked in for our flight. It was the girl's first flight and they were very excited. We had planned to go to Arizona for my graduation, but never thought of a permanent move. This was just confirmation that God was in control.

## Taking the Flight to Phoenix

My girls and I moved to Arizona with about one hundred dollars to our name and about fifty dollars of it went to the airline for oversized baggage. We ate before we got on the plane and ended up eating gummy bears and Chex Mix until we got to our apartment.

## Landing in Phoenix

Four hours later, the plane landed and I saw Monty had texted me. I also saw an e-mail on my phone from my supervisor welcoming me to Phoenix. She said that she would catch up with me about the job in the next two weeks. I took the job because I needed a raise and for the first time in my career, I would be in a leadership position. God knew that I was ready to serve. Two weeks passed, I got the position, but it did not start until January 2016 due to the holiday season.

Once we got to our apartment, it was so cold. I prayed and told God, I am here now, but where's the food? I didn't tell anyone in my family that we were moving because I knew that they wouldn't understand. They had never moved before, but my sole purpose in moving was to get a new life and be obedient to my Heavenly Father.

On that note, I called them to let them know and they were all in shock. I asked them for one hundred dollars so that I could get food for us. Another friend called and sent fifty to help us. That was very unexpected because I knew that he needed to be focused on paying his own bills, but he chose to help me. That's when I realized that he was my friend. I had enough to get groceries, but we needed an air mattress.

The very next day child support came through and was able to buy the rest of what we needed. We still didn't have a car because our 1999 Ford Contour was being shipped to Arizona. I had to make sure that I stayed within my budget to have the funds to get the car. That was my first time having my car shipped and it was quite an experience. When the time came, we got our car and we were rolling throughout the streets of Phoenix.

I think that God loved us moving around during the holiday season because that was exactly what we had been doing for the past two years. All of our furniture was back in Texas with the moving company. It cost a lot to get our belongings, but we survived.

For the first time, I fell in love with our only furniture of air mattresses. We became accustomed to it, but during this time, I learned that we could live on a little and still be happy. When our furniture did arrive, it was so much easier to get rid of things that I had been holding on to because it no longer served a purpose for us.

As a result, some of it was thrown away, but the rest of it was donated to help other families, just like we had been helped during our life transitions.

> I learned that God is my Provider. I shouldn't put any stress on others because God got me covered. I learned that my recognition comes from the Spirit. I learned that God was truly the Prince of Peace. I learned that when people show you, tell you, who they are, believe them right away. You can't change people, but you can make a choice on whether you want them in your space or not.

## The Day It Clicked

I was listening to Youtube to one of my favorite Drake songs and I heard a snippet of a lecture that made me realize what was going on in my love life. The guys that I was choosing to form a connection with had me using my masculine energy. I learned during my healing arts program a great deal about chakras. The chakras are so important in the healing process because the emotions held in each individual chakras speak volumes.

Every human being or living thing has chakras. In a woman, her root chakra is narrow. This means that if she has to worry about paying the bills then her feminine energy is drained. By God's Design, a man is to provide. When this man does not provide then it suppresses the woman and causes problems. So, she is not able to open up her sacral chakra, which is her second chakra, to build him up. I felt like I had won the "Love Lottery" and that's when divine knowledge was bestowed upon me. For the first time in my life, I understood the type of man that I needed. One who was willing, ready, and able to give and receive love.

# Chapter 10:
# Destiny Fulfilled

*I*t's hard to say what the future holds, but I know that God does not renege on his promises and I am willing, ready, and able to receive my inheritance of being a Queen of the Most High. The Bible says it best, *And now, I give you into the care of God and the word of his grace, which is able to make you strong and to give you your heritage among all the saints (Acts 20:32). Giving thanks to the Father, who has qualified us to share in the inheritance of the saints in Light (Colossians 1:12).*

At the end of the day, I learned that faith is everything. When things go south and doors close, don't fret, make a decision to fly and spread your wings, like the Phoenix. Keep the faith and rise according to God's Will for your life. With God, all things are possible and remember, you are loved, valued, and competent.

# Words of Wisdom from Alise

1. You cannot know more about another person than you can know about yourself. And the more you get to know yourself, the better you will understand others.

2. Possessions can possess you. Let go of your attachments to your belongings. I gave up everything I owned and went back to the basics.

3. Sometimes your enemies can help you more than your friends. Enemies are always willing to point out the negative aspects of yourself.

4. Seek to change yourself, not the world first.

5. You can run but you can't Hide.

6. Don't imitate others. Create your own path and walk it out.

7. Never submit yourself to any relationship.

8. True love can never be hurt because it gives without asking anything in return.

9. When you drop all desires and expectations about how people should be, you will never feel deceived or hurt again.

10. Don't be afraid of painful experiences. They can be handled in good and bad ways.

11. Pleasure and pain work together.

12. Don't focus your attention on what people say or do.

13. Own your mess and deal with it.

14. Forgiveness of others and yourself are important. That's how you free yourself.

15. Stay in your own lane and clean the mirrors in your glasshouse. We all live in glasshouses so we shouldn't throw stones. In other words, we should not pass judgement. That's not our calling as the Spirit knows our heart.

## How to Connect with Minister Alise

You can check out the Alise Spiritual Healing & Wellness Center to see how to schedule an intuitive reading, life coaching session, or to just hang out and learn what we are all about. Our website is the following: www.alisehealingcenter.com.

Looking for a guest speaker? Please go the Alise Spiritual Healing & Wellness Center site to invite Alise to speak.

Should you have questions or comments for us, suggestions for future material, or tips, feel free to email us at support@alisehealingcenter.com.

# About the Author

Dr. Alicia Holland is an Intuitive Life Coach, Researcher, and Academic Coach. She is the founder and creator of Alise Spiritual Healing & Wellness Center, a Not-For-Profit, where she coaches with individuals from all walks of life to help them become their best selves and create the lives that they desire.

She travels the world helping others turn their knowledge into a brand by creative passive income and sharing her message: You are Loved, You are Valued, and You are Competent.

Alise lives in Phoenix, Arizona with her family enjoying the beautiful sunrises and sunsets. For more information, visit www.alisehealingcenter.com or www.dr-holland.com.

# About the Alise Spiritual Healing & Wellness Center

We take pride in helping others believe in themselves and go far. As a Not For Profit, Alise Spiritual Healing & Wellness Center's mission is to educate, guide, heal, and empower every individual to become his or her personal best to live a balanced life in body, mind, and spirit. We believe strongly that we are here to help provide spiritual education, guidance, healing, and transformation to help enable people to create positive and lasting changes that will benefit them on their life journey.

Alise Spiritual Healing & Wellness Center is dedicated to providing the best spiritual guidance and upholding the ethics of a wellness holistic practitioner healing practice.

# Notes

# Notes

# Notes

# Notes

# Notes

# Notes

# Notes

# Notes

# Notes

www.ingramcontent.com/pod-product-compliance
Lightning Source LLC
Chambersburg PA
CBHW060714030426
42337CB00017B/2871